Credit Power…
Stay In the Black

Learn How to Maintain an Excellent Credit History.

Learn about the hidden wealth builder that no one talks about. Having an excellent credit can give you access to thousands of unsecure money.

Credit Power… Stay In the Black

Learn How to Maintain an Excellent Credit History.

Learn about the hidden wealth builder that no one talks about. Having an excellent credit can give you access to thousands of unsecure money.

CJ THOMAS

enlighten you. You will learn how to clean up your credit history and promptly build back your trust with lenders in the industry. As a Credit Coach who does group as well as one and one coaching, I can help you understand your credit report, and show you how to rebuild, repair and restore your credit.

After reading kindly e-mail me and let me know how this book has helped you to change your rating from a negative to a positive.

Table of Contents

Introduction

Coming to you from a banking background, one of my previous careers was in Banking, and, I always say that "once a Banker always a Banker". I have worked as a mortgage agent for many years, and over the years of negotiating several mortgages for various clients, I can tell you that I had a difficult time when it comes to getting a mortgage approval for the clients with poor credit rating as opposed to clients with excellent credit.

I can tell you that the clients with poor credit rating suffered emotionally from the stress of not being easily approved for a mortgage, and when they do get an approval, the interest rate they pay is much higher than the clients with excellent credit. Some of my clients had such poor credit ratings that my team and I were unable to secure a mortgage under normal circumstances for those clients. In those cases we have to work miracles to figure out some other alternative for those clients.

I will be the first person to tell you how little I

thought about having a good credit rating –prior to my full understanding about credit and how important it was to my financial life to build and maintain an excellent credit. I was one of those people who told the collection agencies to go ahead and add the current bill they were calling me about to all the other unpaid bills I had at the credit bureau.

I did not care about my credit history because I didn't know any better. Maya Angelou said, "When you know better you do better". No one ever really sat me down and taught me about the importance of maintaining a good credit history. I was not educated about how credit really works. Prior to the first-hand experience I suffered from having a poor credit, I had no clue that when you have an excellent credit it's like you have access to a gold mine.

Looking back now, I still can't believe I actually told the collection agents that it was not going to make a difference to me if the unpaid bill was added to my credit report or not. I soon realize how wrong I was, and how it would affect my overall credit health. All my bills that went to collections negatively affected my credit rating for several years.

The irresponsible credit decisions I made, negatively affected my financial life, and it caused me to lose a lot of money from paying a much higher interest rate on credit products. Although it was a very bad call on my part, when my credit got ruined, it was like a blessing in disguise. I have learnt my lessons along the way which have proven quite valuable. I eventually turned my negative experiences into positive which now makes me able to help others.

My clients can now learn how to treat their credit as if it's a gold mine, and it is. I teach them how not to make the same credit mistakes I made. It took me a long time to get my credit back on track and now I guard my credit like a high quality gold bar.

When you know the value of having an excellent credit history, then you are aware that not only can it increase your self-worth, but it can give you access to a lot of unsecured money. This is money that is not secured against any physical asset like a house or a car. I can imagine that many of you have no idea that when you have an excellent credit rating it will give you the power to create massive wealth for yourself.

Your credit report is basically all your credit habits – good or bad it is collected and stored to create your credit history. This information becomes the tool that can be used by lenders and creditors to assess your creditworthiness. Although your credit report signifies a good portion of your credit history, this data is not saved for the length of your credit life. Your credit information is eventually removed from your credit report to make room for new credit reporting.

How to Build, Manage and Maintain Excellent Credit Rating

It is very important to have a good credit rating, especially these days for a number of reasons. More and more services/companies are using your credit rating as a deal breaker in their decision making. Some companies will check your credit to see how well you have managed your financial responsibilities in the past, in order to measure how responsible you are. Accordingly, lenders will use your bad credit history as a reason to charge you a higher interest rate; this is if they decide to advance you any credit at all.

Your credit rating will be checked when applying for these services:
- Credit Card
- Loan (including business loan and car loan)
- Lines of credit
- Overdraft protection
- Mortgage

- Apartment and business rental
- Debit machine for your business
- Student loan (in some cases)
- Work (it depends on your field of work.)

What is credit?

Credit means receiving something of value now and promising to pay for it at a later date. A financial charge is often added by the lender to the principal amount borrowed. American and Canadian consumers use credit to buy almost everything. This includes food, clothing, housing and transportation.

The Rules of Credit
The rules of credit are few and simple. A lender extends a credit product, the agreement would be to repay the lender the amount you received plus interest charges and possible additional service fees. The lender will then prepare a payment schedule, according to which you are required to make payments. With this in mind, the most important advice is "pay your bills on time"

Who is a creditor?
A creditor is the party to whom a debt is owed; it is the supplier of credit to an individual or a business. For example, a creditor is a person, bank, or other

organization that has lent money, extended credit or supplied service to another party.

Who is a Lender?

A Lender makes funds available to someone with the expectation that the funds will be repaid, plus any interest or fees. A Lender can be an individual, a public or private group, who may provide funds for a variety of reasons, for example: line of credit, automobile, mortgage, personal or small business loan.

Who Is a Borrower?

A Borrower initially receives or borrows an amount of money or credit of some kind from the lender. The Borrower borrows for an automobile, mortgage, loan etc. with the intention to pay the principal amount back with interest; the interest is to compensate the lender for borrowing.

Who Is a Debtor?

A debtor can be a person, an entity or a company who owes money to someone else. Therefore a debtor has a debt or legal obligation to pay an amount that is owed to another person or entity. For example, if you borrow money from a bank, you are the debtor and the bank is the lender for the duration of the loan or until the loan is repaid in full.

What is the principal loan amount?

The principal amount is the original amount of the mortgage or loan before the interest is added. So, the principal amount plus the interest is the obligation that is to be paid back in full or repay in an equal amount of money to the lender at a later time.

Credit Risk

The Credit risk is simply defined as the possible risk the creditor has to endure if a borrower fails to meet their financial obligations in accordance with the agreed terms.

Credit Risk Management

Credit Risk Management is a critical component of a complete approach to risk management. The goal of Credit Risk Management is to maximize a bank's risk-adjusted rate of return by maintaining credit risk exposure within a satisfactory parameter.

What is Risk Assessment?

Risk Assessment is a general term used across many industries to determine the likelihood of loss of an asset, loan, or investment. Evaluating the risk is essential for lenders to determine if an investment is worthwhile, so they try to ensure the best process to minimize the risk. It also determines the rate of return necessary to ensure a particular investment is successful.

When lending for personal loans, lines of credit, and mortgages the lender will also conduct risk assessments, known as credit checks. For example, it is common that lenders do not approve borrowers who have credit scores below 600 because lower scores are symbolic of poor credit practices. A lender's credit analysis may consider other factors, such as investments that can be easily turned into liquid cash, collateral, property, income, or cash on hand.

Credit Analysis

The objective of performing a credit analysis is to look at both the borrower and the lending facility being proposed, and to assign a risk rating. Credit analyst gathers and analyzes financial data, such as the purpose of the loan, the borrower's payment history, liabilities, earnings, assets and other information for warning signs that might present financial risks. This is the method by which the credit analyst calculates the creditworthiness of an individual, business or organization.

Who is an A-Lender?

The A-lender is a traditional lender servicing the A-client. The A-clients are equipped with an excellent credit score. The institutions servicing the A-clienteles include Canada's six major banks; these are Bank of Nova Scotia (Scotiabank), National Bank of Canada, Bank of Montreal (BMO), Canadian Imperial Bank of Commerce (CIBC), Toronto-Dominion Bank (TD), and Royal Bank of Canada (RBC). When it comes to credit products, these banks only cater to customers with good credit scores and a reliable income.

Who is a B-Lender?

The B-Lenders don't have to go through the huge qualification hurdle like the-A-lenders. The B-Lenders have basically lowered the entry level for you to qualify for their products. This leniency in the qualification process is offset with a higher interest rate.

With that said, these B-Lenders usually cater to people who may not qualify for a mortgage or a credit card at one of Canada's big six banks, because of these factors: New immigrants, weak credit rating, no credit history, and non-guaranteed income; for example, if an individual is self-employed their income is not guaranteed.

Here are the names of a few B-lenders servicing the-B-Clientele;

- Home Trust,
- Equitable Bank, and
- Home Capital Group.

If you have to accept a credit product from a B-

Lender, it is very essential to take a good look at the conditions the B-Lenders are offering; this is to ensure that you will not get trapped with a high interest rate you cannot afford.

How to Start Building Credit

I will speak to you from a Canadian credit standpoint because I am living in Canada. When it comes to credit and credit score, the mortgage and loan rules are pretty much the same in most countries. In Canada, however, when you open a bank account in most banks, based on your credit rating, the banks will immediately check your credit to see if you would be qualified for a credit card. And, if your account is a checking account, you might be immediately offered an overdraft protection. When you receive your credit card bill, the minimum balance must be paid on or before the due date. Keep reading and, you will find some more in-depth information about the best and fastest way to build your credit.

What is an Overdraft Protection

An overdraft protection is a guaranteed service that the bank will cover cheques up to the maximum of the overdraft amount. Basically, even if there are insufficient funds in the holder's account to cover the debit, the bank will use the overdraft protection to clear the transaction regardless.

When a person uses their debit card or bank cheque to make a purchase, if the purchase exceeds the amount in their checking account, typically that purchase would be declined. However when you have the overdraft protection in place, it is like having an insurance to guarantee that your obligation will be paid up to your overdraft protection amount.

This is because the individual's bank or credit union will provide the additional funds necessary to cover the transaction.

Note: *Although overdraft protection is handy to have, it comes with additional fees and charges. You will only be qualified for this if you have a good* *credit rating.*

The Basic Types of Consumer Credit Are:
- Non-installment Credit.
- Installment Closed-end Credit.
- Revolving Open-end Credit.

Non-instalment Credit: This type of credit is the simplest to understand. It is usually a short-term credit that is offered for a term of use, more than likely a term of thirty (30) days. It is a loan that is repaid all at once, and it is paid in a single payment. This short-term credit typically doesn't let the borrower pay any interest.

Instalment credit: This type is best explained when there is a loan agreement, and the terms of repayment agreement is to repay it with interest in instalments of a specified amount over the life of the loan. The pre-set life of the loan could usually range anywhere from months to years.
Loans are therefore instalment credit. Therefore if you have a mortgage or a car loan, they are classified as instalment credit. Instalment credit is probably the most commonly used and easiest form of credit to understand.

Revolving credit: This type of credit is open-ended. When the money you borrow has no end date for repayment, instead, the agreement is to repay a certain minimum amount each month, which will

carry a balance. In this case you can borrow
additional funds up to a pre-set limit each month.
The longer the principal of the debt remains
unpaid, the more interest you'll be charged on the
remaining balance. Credit cards are the most
common form of revolving credit.

Credit Card- Credit cards are often the most used
and most accepted forms of credit. It actually gives
the user access to upfront monies that the credit
card holder is billed for monthly. Banks, retail
stores, businesses and credit card companies
provide a wide variety of credit cards that you can
apply for.

Note: *Ensure to examine the terms and conditions
of your credit card closely, this is because creditors
do charge interest that can rapidly increase your
credit card balance if it's not kept under control.*

Secured Credit and Unsecured Credit - These two
types of credits are distinguished by two factors…

The Secured Credit - A secured credit card is a
safer option for lenders. This type of credit card lets
the borrower provide the funds up front, and it can
allow a person to both establish and build their

credit all at the same time, this is all done without any preapproval.

A secured credit can be a revolving or a non-revolving credit, and it can be of various types of credit products. These products can range anywhere from: Credit cards, loans, lines of credit and mortgages. In the case of a mortgage, it is always backed by the mortgagee's property. Basically, the house is used as collateral in case the borrower forfeits on the mortgage payment, the lender will take position of the mortgaged property for payment. Some secured lines of credit are also secured by a house as collateral. The house used as collateral is the reason the line of credit was approved in the first place.

Note: *All secured credit lines will charge an annual fee, so watch for it and make sure you understand the terms and conditions attached to it. The secured line of credit will involve a signed agreement to give the lender permission to seize a particular asset from the borrower if they default on their payments.*

Unsecured credit – Whether the loan is revolving or non-revolving there are no collateral required for unsecured credit. The lenders will approve your application based on a few key factors. The number one and most important is your credit rating, they want to see how well you managed your credit history. The next one is the length of employment, and then your annual income. These precautions are taken by the lender to analyze the risk factor for repayment.

How to Get Your First Credit Card or How to Repair Your Credit

Getting your first credit card or fixing your credit is more important now-a-days than ever before. One of the reasons for this significant push for you to establish your credit as soon as possible is because 35 percent of the credit score is based on your payment history, so a huge percentage of your credit score is based on the length of your credit and how well you managed your credit over time.

If you don't establish a credit you will not be able to get a mortgage, so basically you are unintentionally holding yourself back from creating wealth. The new mortgage rule in Canada makes it very difficult for new home buyers to enter the housing market. If one of your goal is to own your own home, you will definitely need to have an established credit in order to qualify for a mortgage. As mentioned before, the length of your payment history is a key component when it comes to establishing your credit, and as well, it affects your credit score.

The credit score in Canada range anywhere from 300 to 900, and the higher your credit score is, the better your chances are of being approved for loans and other credit products. In general, a score of 650 and above is considered good and it shows that you are less likely to default on loans; you are then seen as a good candidate to be approved for credit.

A credit score of 750 or higher is considered an excellent credit. In most cases, a minimum score of 680 is required for a mortgage approval for most A Lenders, such as banks and other traditional financial institutions. Credit scores of 600 or below are unfortunately considered low, and lenders will see you as a high risk borrower.

A lot of A-Lenders, especially banks, will have strict policies about the clients they consider to be approved for mortgages and the ones they consider as risky. So, for someone with a credit score under 600, application will have to be made to a B-Lender for credit consideration.

With all that in mind, you will need to start to build your credit as soon as you can, and the easiest way for you to obtain credit is to start by applying for a credit card. If you have a poor or a bad credit, you will need to build trust again in the credit industry, so you will have to start by applying for a secured credit card. There are a number of banks that offer secure credit cards. However, you can get a secured credit card from anyone of the following companies: Capital One, Home Trust and Refresh Financial to name a few.

Keep in mind that credit cards are revolving credit and the minimum payment must be paid monthly and on time. The minimum payment must be paid on or before the due date in order to be ranked favorably in the credit bureau. With that said, if you have a bad credit, you will have to repair your credit rating before you can be approved for an unsecure credit card. If your credit is poor, you will have to apply for a secured credit card, a secured credit card will help you to rebuild your credit.

Benefits of Having an Excellent Credit

Here are some of the reasons you should keep your credit in good standing. When you have an excellent credit rating, you are always guaranteed to get the best interest rate for credit products like these:

- Mortgage
- Motor vehicle loan
- Credit card
- Personal loan and business loan
- Line of credit

When you apply for any credit product, the creditor's decision will depend on your credit rating/profile. The credit analyst will take everything into consideration when doing the risk assessment to see if you qualify for credit. The risk management analyze the amount of risk that the lender will or will not have to endure, and based on their findings, (if you are approved), is how your interest payment will be set.

Your credit report history and your credit score will

tell the lender how well you have managed your financial responsibilities over a certain period of time. You will be rewarded for managing your credit in a responsible manner, and having a good credit report and credit score will give you the ability to save a lot of money by paying a lower interest on credit products. Your excellent credit allows you the opportunity to get an unsecured line of credit that can be used to start a business or even purchase an investment property.

The cost of borrowing is very expensive and even more so if you don't have a good credit rating. A good credit doesn't only save you money by having a lower interest rate, but it can help to build generational wealth by accessing an unsecured line of credit or to get a business loan. These are some of the reasons it's important that you build and maintain an excellent credit.

It takes a little while for you to be able to build your credit history, so I would suggest that you should get started right away. I can guarantee you that an excellent credit can positively change your financial future.

Mortgage Renewal - If you already have a mortgage, it will have to be renewed from time to time, when you have an excellent credit it will give you the bargaining power needed to get the best interest rate from your current lender. Your excellent credit will definitely give you an edge in the renegotiating process. It will give you the opportunity to get the best interest rate possible for your mortgage renewal.

Your lender will recognize that with your excellent credit, you can walk into any A-lender's establishment and secure a mortgage, knowing this... Your lender is more than likely to get you the best interest rate they have to offer. This is because they know that you can switch to any A-Lender without having to pay a penalty as long as your mortgage is up for renewal.

Now you realize that when you have an excellent credit rating it also gives you choices, you have the choice to be able to shop around to other lenders for the best interest rate available. Thus, when you have an excellent credit it puts you in the driver's seat with the lender. That said, it is in your current lender's best interest to negotiate the best rate available for your mortgage.

Credit reporting agencies in Canada

There are two national credit bureaus in Canada:
- Equifax Canada
- TransUnion Canada.

I would suggest that you should check your credit from time to time with both agencies. The reason for this is to see if you are in agreement with what is reported on your credit report. If you notice any discrepancies on your report, you can dispute it, and get the credit reporting agency to correct the errors.

In most cases, you will notice an increase in your credit score once the errors on your credit report has been corrected. Credit errors on your credit report can negatively affect your credit score, so it is in your best interest to ensure that you are in agreement with everything showing on your credit report.

Although personal information such as the correct

spelling of your name, address, and the correct job information will not affect your credit score, it is still important to ensure that all errors are corrected. Equifax Canada is more popular for lenders to report to than TransUnion Canada; therefore most lenders will check your credit with Equifax Canada. Nonetheless, I would suggest that you should check your credit report from both TransUnion and Equifax.

In May of 2018, the province of Ontario passed legislation to improve fairness in credit reporting. This new law will give Ontario consumers the strongest rights in Canada over information held by the consumer reporting agencies.

The access to consumer credit report requires certain credit reporting agencies to:

- Give consumers free online access to their credit report and current credit score at least two times per year.
- Include in a consumer report, any credit scores given to third parties in the past twelve (12) months.
- Implement a credit freeze at the request of a consumer, to help reduce identity theft.

You can check your credit report on-line as often as you like but, after your free copies for the year you will be charged a fee. You can also go to the credit reporting agency office to check your credit there; the fee is much cheaper when you check your credit at the credit reporting office as opposed to checking it on-line. Nonetheless, both credit bureaus offer free credit report.

For those of you who are ordering your free credit report by mail, you will have to wait for up to three weeks to receive your free credit report. There is a verification process whereby you will have to send in two pieces of identification, as well as some basic background information.

Note: *Every time a creditor pulls your credit report you lose some point from your credit score, when the creditor pulls your credit it is called a hard copy, there is not much you can do about it if you are trying to apply for a credit product. However, you won't lose any points if you pull your own credit report online or at the credit reporting office, and your credit score will not be affected. This type of inquiry is called a soft copy. If you are applying for a credit product, the creditor will still have to pull their own credit report on you for their file.*

Note: *Creditors will sometimes pull a soft copy without your knowledge.*

Tips for Building Your Credit

Always make your payments on time - Pay at least your minimum payment on or before the due date. In order to manage your debts properly and responsibly, it is recommended that you should pay more than the minimum monthly payment so that you can pay off your balance quicker.

If possible pay the full amount of your balance during the grace period and you won't be charged any interest charges. Grace periods are typically between 21 and 27 days, and most credit card companies do have a grace period.

If you can afford to pay off your credit card balance monthly, it would mean that you are borrowing money for free. Keep in mind that if you can pay your full balance monthly, you still have to pay it on or before the due date. If your balance is paid in full each month your creditor won't be making any money from you. This should make you very happy as you are able to borrow money without paying any interest, but they won't be happy because they are not making any interest payment from you as a customer.

You don't have to feel sorry for your credit card company because they have enough customers carrying a monthly balance that will make up for the few people who are able to pay off their credit card balances without paying the interest payment.

Don't over extend your credit limit, maxing out on your available credit limit can be damaging to your credit rating, So, keep an eye on your credit limit and don't exceed your limit. I would suggest you stay within that 30% credit utilization, and your credit score will drastically increase.

Create a payment system so it can help you to monitor your credit account, you could create a payment reminder on your phone, your computer, write it on your day timer, or on your calendar. Ensure to have a payment budget, when you plan your payment schedule, this will help you to manage your money as well.

Fees: Some credit cards will charge you an annual fee, which can be as high as $59.00. If an annual fee is charged it is in addition to the annual interest rate. You can negotiate for your credit card company to waive your annual fee. They might comply after the careful review of your credit account to ensure that you have maintained your credit card in good standing.

Other Fees: Some of these fees are applied at the end of your billing period based on your credit usage:

Over limit charge – this is charged once your account balance exceeds your credit limit at any given time during the billing period.

Dishonoured payment/Cheque – There is a fee charged if you have a preauthorized payment bounced due to "insufficient funds". This means that you went over your credit limit, so there is no money left on your card to make the payment. A non-sufficient fund (NSF), can sometimes happen when your credit card is hooked up to your PayPal account and you make a purchase using PayPal. PayPal can sometimes take a few days to post the payment on their end.

Therefore if you are not keeping track of your credit card transactions, you can easily forget about that pending debit amount. In this case you are charged both the over limit amount, and the dishonoured payment amount. It is not fair by any means, but this is a way for the credit card company to keep your focus on your finances.

Cash advanced – some credit card companies will

charge you a fee for cash advanced. Cash advanced is when you used your credit card to obtain physical cash. When the credit card is used to make purchases you do have the grace period to make the payment before any interest charge is applied. If you take a cash advance off your credit card, the interest charges will start on the day you take the cash advance.

As I mentioned prior, that interest on credit cards are only charged when you are carrying a balance. When used properly, a credit card can be a very good friend because you can borrow to purchase the things you need today, and pay it back later without interest if you take advantage of the grace period and pay the balance in full. And the bonus is that you get to build your credit in the process.

Note - *If you are paying your credit card bill on the actual due date, you should not mail the payment to the credit card company, because if you do that it will be posted to your account when they receive it which is after the due date. If that happens, you will be hit with the interest charges, plus it will show negatively on your credit report. It will be shown as a late payment, and it will definitely affects your credit.*

If you forget to pay your credit card bill on or before the due date, my advice is to pay it as soon as you remember to avoid charges. Once your bill is past due 30 days, 60 days, 90 days, and 120 days , the credit card company will send it to a collection agency, this is after the credit card company have tried and fail to collect from you. When this happens it will definitely put you in the category of a bad debtor, and you will have a bad credit rating. Your bad debt will last for six to seven years on your credit report; take it from me when I tell you that it's not worth it. So, if you run into any credit difficulties with your credit card payment, you should speak to your creditor as soon as possible, and make payment arrangement with them. Most creditors are very reasonable, and will work with you. You have to remember that the creditors want to be paid, so they are willing to work with you.

Become an Authorized User
When you become an authorized user it can help to build your credit more rapidly– Once you become an authorized user on someone else's credit card, you will automatically assume the credit card holder's credit history. This is the fastest and the most effective strategy you can use to build your credit.

Here Are the Pros and Cons of Being an

Authorized User

Pros – When you become an authorized user on someone's credit card, it can catapult you into having an excellent credit history, alongside that individual. You should always ensure that the individual who gave you the authorization on their credit card has a worthy card habit. The bills are paid on-time, and they have a low debt-to-credit ratio. This individual's good credit rating will be reflected on your credit report, and it will help you to build an effective credit history in a very short time.

Cons- If the card holder has an unfavorable credit history, such as a high debt-to credit-ratio, late payments and collections, the authorized user will inherit that negative credit history. Although this is a great way to achieve an instant credit history, this option should be done with caution. You should ensure that the card holder is a responsible creditor, and the credit utilization is at 10%.

Note – If you are adding someone to your credit card as an authorized user to help this person to improve on their credit, you don't have to give them an actual credit card for them to use. It is totally up to you and the relationship you have with the person; it depends on how well you know and trust the individual. It all depends on who the person is to you, and your history with him/her. It is important to know that an authorized user has no legal obligation to repay the credit card debt.

Know that whenever he or she uses the credit card to make purchases it is your responsibility to ensure the money is repaid. After all, it is your excellent credit that is on the line, and you cannot turn the power of maintaining your credit over to someone else. I would suggest you don't issue a physical credit card to this individual. After a few months of their names reporting to the credit bureau, they can go ahead and apply for their very own credit card.

Adding an individual as a Joint Account Holder – If someone is added to the credit card account as a joint account holder, that person has a legal obligation to pay the credit card balance. If the balance is not paid by either party, it can ruin both joint account holder credit rating.

A Credit Guarantor

This option has to be done with caution. I actually don't recommend that you become a guarantor for just about anyone. The reason for my opinion is that the bank is issuing the credit product to this individual based on you the guarantor's good credit. If for any reason this person decides to forfeit on the loan, the guarantor is on the hook for the balance owing.

This is the reason the lender ensures that guarantors have a good credit and is willing to assume financial responsibility for the individual. If this debt is not paid by either party it will ruin the guarantor's good credit rating, and it can also ruin your relationship with each other. I certainly don't recommend this option, but I still want you to be aware of the risk involve.

Tips–Manage Your Credit Card to Build Credit

If you are trying to build your credit, and you are approved for a credit card, as soon as you receive your credit card you should activate your card and start using it immediately. The reason you want to start using your credit card right away is because you want to get into the credit reporting system as soon as you can.

This is a system that keeps track of your payment history, it keeps track that you make your payment on the date agreed upon. When all your bills are paid on time it means that you are building a good credit rating and you are proving to creditors that you are creditworthy, and that you can be trusted. Equifax Canada and TransUnion Canada will start to track your credit activities to create a history in their system about your credit and payment behavior. Knowing this information, it is vital for you to ensure that you are creating an excellent credit history. Besides, the length of your great credit history helps to increase your credit score.

If you are not qualified for a credit card from the bank because you are a new creditor who has never had credit before, or if you had a poor credit rating for whatever reason. It is not the end of the world; you can still obtain a credit card, by simply applying for a Secured credit card. It is very important to know that paying off the balance is not as important to build your credit as paying your minimum monthly payment on time.

Credit Can Affect Your Qualification for Other Monthly Bills

You might be surprise to learn that a good credit is needed to acquire some utility services. You do recognize that you are billed after you have used one month of utilities – so the utility companies are always loaning you 30 days' worth of utilities in advance. This is the reason, the companies will check to see if you have a good credit rating before turning on your utilities. This applies to most utility services including gas, electricity, water, and even some cell phone providers.

Since your credit is defined by how well you have managed and paid your bills in the past, a lot of businesses such as: Landlords, mortgage lenders, and even some employers will use your credit to predict your future financial behavior. If you need to borrow money, or if you need a variety of services, your credit will be taken into consideration prior to the extension of credit. These are some of the reasons you have to maintain a good credit.

Mortgage Application and Credit Lines – When you apply for a mortgage, the lender will want to know that you have at least three credit lines. This shows that you have at least three credit products that you are managing properly. The mortgage lender feels more confident that you are creditworthy when you can responsibly manage three or more credit lines. An excellent credit is one of the major factors for you to be approved for a mortgage by A-lenders.

What makes up your credit score?
Five components that make up your credit score:

Length of credit history is 15%: Your rating takes into consideration how long you've had credit or how long you've been paying bills. If you are new to the country or you are a young adult, you will have little or no credit history.

Payment history is 35%: The biggest factor that makes up your score is how well you've managed your bill payments over the history of your credit life; this is whether you paid by instalments in full and on time.

Credit utilization is 30%: Maxing out on your available credit can be detrimental to your credit rating. For example, if your credit card's limit is $3,000 and you are using $2100, this means that you are using 70% of the available credit. Your score will be lower than if your utilization is under 30% the recommended usage.

New loans or applications 10%: If you applied for frequent loans, your credit score will be negatively impacted, so only apply for what you actually need.

Varied credit is 10%: Your last piece of credit rating is your various types of credit. If you have not had more than one type of credit, your rating will be lower than if you have had a mixture of different types of credit products.

The Duration of Credit Information on Credit Report
In Canada, creditors and lenders usually report to Equifax and or TransUnion, these are the two credit reporting bureaus in Canada. The credit reporting bureaus usually create a credit report on all borrowers, and this report is used by creditors and lenders to assess the creditworthiness of a potential borrower.

The Timeline for Credit Account Paid off In Good Standing
The Credit accounts that are paid off on time and are in good standing will continue to remain on your credit report for twenty (20) years after the last day the account was active. This paid off old

account is great for your credit history, it shows potential future lenders that you are a responsible borrower. It is always good to have a positive lengthy credit history, and the way to create this is by being responsible in paying your loans.

The Delinquent Credit Accounts Timeline

It would be great for your credit report history if the delinquent or other unfavorable information is remove as soon as possible; this is because these are the types of information that will lower your credit score, and will hinder you from getting approved for the credit products you desire. Nonetheless, the negative credit information does stay on your credit report so that creditors and lenders can use it to assess your risk level. However you will be happy to know that the negative credit information does not stay on your credit report for as long as the positive credit information. The credit delinquent information timeline differ in the two different credit bureaus. The good news is that the debt will eventually disappear from your credit history, in most cases. Equifax and Trans Union only keep record of delinquent amounts for six to seven years from the last payment or default date. Here is a detailed list of how long the different types of negative credit information will stay on your report.

Equifax & TransUnion

Credit cards, lines of credit and loans	6 years
A secured loan backed by an asset	6 years
(NSF)	6 years
Closed chequing or savings accounts due to fraud	6 years
Enquiry	3 years
Enquiry – TransUnion	6 years
Legal judgments	6 years

TransUnion keeps legal judgment information for:

Ontario, Quebec, New Brunswick, Newfoundland and Labrador	7 years
P.E.I.	10 years
Accounts in Collection	6 years
Liens	6 years
Lien – TransUnion	5 years
Bankruptcy	6 years

TransUnion keeps bankruptcy information for:

Ontario, Quebec, New Brunswick, Newfoundland Labrador, and P.E.I.	7 years
Multiple bankruptcies	14 years
Consumer proposal	3 years

It is essential to know that the two credit reporting bureaus, Equifax and TransUnion, keep credit information for different amounts of time. As well, some creditors report to only one bureau, therefore if you only request a copy from one of the two bureaus, some information may not appear on your credit report.

Statute of limitations

The Canadian legislation sets a statute of limitations on unsecured debt. This statute of limitations prevents creditors or collection agency from taking debtors to court after a certain amount of time has passed. This calculation starts from the time you made your last payment on the debt. The number of years are different across provinces and territories as follows:

Alberta	2 years
British Columbia	2 years
Manitoba	6 years
New Brunswick	2 years
Newfoundland and Labrador	6 years
Nova Scotia	6 years
Ontario	2 years
Prince Edward Island	6 years

Quebec	3 years
Saskatchewan	2 years
The territories	6 years

When your creditors are unable to take legal action it means that they won't have the means to garnish your wages. The debt collection agencies will not stop harassing you, and they might even continue to threaten to sue you. This is because they know that most debtors will not know the law enough to realize that it is an empty threat.

CREDIT POWER... Stay In the Black
+ Black = Good
- Red   = Bad
Excellent Credit = Wealth

Request a copy of your credit report from:
Equifax Canada
1-800-465-7166
consumer.relations@equifax.ca
TransUnion Canada
1-877-713-3393
(Quebec only)
1-800-663-9980
(All other provinces)
marketing@tuc.ca

My Contact Information

I am a Credit Coach and a Life Coach

Email:
cjthomasmgnt@gmail.com

Twitter:
twitter.com/cjthomasmgnt

Facebook:
https://business.facebook.com/
Cj-Thomas-Mgnt-273938056528458/

YouTube:
www.youtube.com/channel/
UCfAW19sbtPfnM5P8zZp16Uw?
view_as=subscriber

Instagram:
https://www.instagram.com/cthomasmgnt/